The Book of American
Trade Marks/10
The Annual of Trade Mark Design

David E. Carter

First Printing, 1987
Second Printing, 1990

ART DIRECTION BOOK COMPANY
10 East 39th Street
New York, New York 10016

212/889-6500

Library of Congress Catalog Card Number: 72-76493
International Standard Book Number: 088108-034-9
ISBN for Standing Orders for this series: 0910158-38-X

How to submit marks for future volumes.

This book is part of a series which shows good examples of contemporary design of trade marks, corporate symbols and logos.

Designers are invited to submit marks for possible inclusion in future volumes. Work submitted must adhere to the following guidelines:

(1) marks must be sent in the actual size they are to be reproduced in the book. Any marks not meeting this standard will be eliminated from consideration.

(2) do not mount the work.

(3) include the name of the client, and the one name to appear in the credit line as designer.

(4) send a letter giving permission for the marks to be included in the book.

Due to the large amount of material received each year, it is impossible for us to acknowledge receipt of marks.

All material should be sent to David E. Carter, Trade Marks, P.O. Box 2500, Ashland, Kentucky 41105-2500.

9465

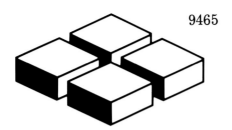

9469

Maids to Go

9466

9470

DURADENT
C O R P O R A T I O N

9467

Golden State Guides

9471

VEAL CONNECTION CORP.

9468

▴ BJL ▴ INTERIOR ▴ DESIGN ▴

9472

OAK MOUNTAIN
PROPERTY MANAGEMENT CO., INC.

9473

Tierra Cast Findings

9474

9475

9476

9480

9477

9481

9478

9482

9479

9483

9484

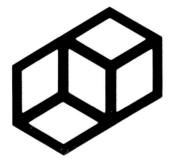

9485

9486

9487

9491

9488

9492

9489

9493

9490

9494

9495

9496

9497

9487   National Bank Of The Redwoods
            Designer: Lynn Ostling

9488   Orestes Golden Bear
            Designer: Lynn Ostling

9489   Printery
            Designer: Scott Hull

9490   Colonial City Aviation
            Designer: Scott Hull

9491   Scott Hull
            Designer: Scott Hull

9492   Zaccagnini Greenhouse & Nursery
            Designer: Scott Hull

9493   Danville Jaycees
            Designer: Scott Hull

9494   Jeff Friedman Photography
            Designer: Scott Hull

9495   Hulls Barber Shop
            Designer: Scott Hull

9496   R.A. Bergs, Inc.
            Designer: Scott Hull

9497   Brown and Williamson (Proposed)
            Designer:Scott Hull

9498

HULL'S SPORTSWEAR SHOP

27495 Flat Run Road
Danville, Ohio 43014
Phone (614) 599-6690

9502

Salsa

9499

WANAMAKER
WIDOW MAKERS

9503

Las Vegas Live

9500

ED WORKMAN
REALTY

9504

DAWSON
CONSTRUCTION

9501

Alpine

9505

Skyview

9506

9507

9508

9498	Hulls Sportswear Shop Designer: Scott Hull
9499	Wanamaker Advertising Designer: Scott Hull
9500	Ed Workman Realty Designer: Scott Hull
9501	Alpine Designer: Scott Hull
9502	Brown and Williamson (Proposed) Designer: Scott Hull
9503	Wear-Ever (Proposed) Designer: Scott Hull
9504	Dawson Construction Designer: Scott Hull
9505	Skyview Condominiums-Birm., Alabama Designer: Richard E. Lyons
9506	The Harbor, Sandusky, Ohio Designer: Richard E. Lyons
9507	Lenora Jackson, Ltd. Designer: Richard E. Lyons
9508	Seasons, The Steak Club Designer: Richard E. Lyons

9509

9513

9510

9514

9511

9515

9512

9516

9517

fallschase

9518

9519

9520

9524

9521

9525

9522

9526

9523

9527

9528

9529

JAGDISH J. CHAVDA

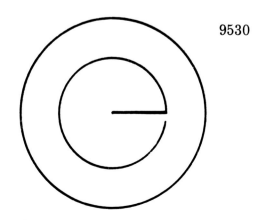

9530

9520   Nife Rest, Inc.
        Designer: Richard E. Lyons

9521   Carmel Condominiums
        Designer: Richard E. Lyons

9522   Laffites Restaurant & Lounge

        Designer: Richard E. Lyons

9523   Quadrum
        Designer: Richard E. Lyons

9524   Regency Crown Condominiums
        Designer: Richard E. Lyons

9525   Sibley Forest
        Designer: Richard E. Lyons

9526   Buckhead Beef
        Designer: Richard E. Lyons

9527   Charter Clinic, Inc.
        Designer: Richard E. Lyons

9528   Rosthema, Ltd., Interiors
        Designer: Richard E. Lyons

9529   Jagdish J. Chavda
        Designer: Jagdish J. Chavda

9530   Ozair Esmail
        Designer: Jagdish J. Chavda

9531

9535

Bajamar

9532

KEY WEST
REFLECTIONS

9536

Outlook

9533

bien venidos a
SAN AGUSTIN

9537

Ciudad de MEXICO

9534

NEW ORLEANS
and all that jazz

9538

THE ALLIGATOR
Disgusting Monster of Our Swamps

9539

9540

9531	Helen Hiers Designer: Jagdish J. Chavda
9532	Gra-Pix Designer: Jagdish J. Chavda
9533	Gra-Pix Designer: Jagdish J. Chavda
9534	Gra-Pix Designer: Jagdish J. Chavda
9535	Gra-Pix Designer: Jagdish J. Chavda
9536	NPN Corporation dpa Outlook Designer: Jagdish J. Chavda
9537	Gra-Pix Designer: Jagdish J. Chavda
9538	The Florida Naturalist: Florida Audubon Society Designer: Jagdish J. Chavda
9539	Joanne Hutchinson Assocs., Interior Design Designer: Carol Anne Ganno
9540	Encinitas German Auto Service Designer: Carol Anne Ganno
9541	University of California, San Diego, Libraries Designer: Carol Anne Ganno

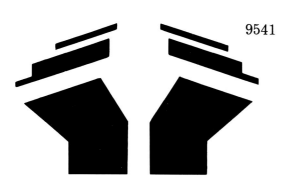

9541

9542

9546

9543

9547

9544

9548

9545

9549

9550

STUDIOGRAPHIX

9551

AFFILIATED CLUBS AND RESTAURANTS, INC.

9552

9542   William Assocs., Architecture
Designer: Carol Anne Ganno

9543   Lentz & Assocs., Inc., Interior
Design
Designer: Carol Anne Ganno

9544   Flying Boat-Ben Lexcen, Yacht
Design
Designer: Carol Anne Ganno

9545   Eclipse-Ben Lexcen, Yacht Design
Designer: Carol Anne Ganno

9546   Gold River Casino
Designer: Carol Anne Ganno

9547   Gerald Garapich Assocs.,
Architects
Designer: Carol Anne Ganno

9548   Otto's Deli-Restaurant
Designer: Bob Mynster/Studio
Graphix

9549   The Plaza Pastry Shop
Designer: Bob Mynster/Studio
Graphix

9550   Studio Graphix
Designer: Bob Mynster/Studio
Graphix

9551   Affiliated Clubs & Restaurants
Inc.
Designer: Bob Mynster/Studio
Graphix

9552   Sibley & Wolff
Designer: Bob Mynster/Studio
Graphix

9553

TROJAN OIL PRODUCTION AND SERVICES, INC

9557

9554

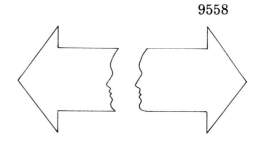

9558

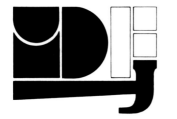

9555

9559

9556

9560

9561

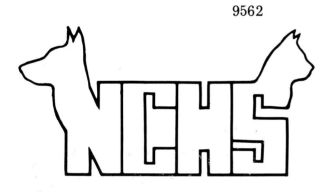

9562

9563

9553	Trojan Oil Company Designer: Tom Taber/Studio Graphix
9554	McKinney Avenue Market Designer: Joanne T. West
9555	Your Design Furniture Designer: Joanne T. West
9556	Grocery Supply, Inc. Designer: Joanne T. West
9557	Franklin Electronics Designer: Joanne T. West
9558	Schizophrenia Inst. of Texas Designer: Joanne T. West
9559	Julien Devereux and Friends Designer: Joanne T. West
9560	The Purveyors Designer: Joanne T. West
9561	Twin House Communications Designer: Joanne T. West
9562	Navarro County Humane Society Designer: Joanne T. West
9563	Medical Arts Clinic Designer: Joanne T. West

9564

9568

9565

9569

9566

9570

9567

9571

9572

9573

9574

9564 West Brand, Inc.
      Designer: Joanne T. West

9565 Crown Distributors, Inc.
      Designers: Joanne T. West

9566 Texas Resource Group, Inc.
      Designer: Joanne T. West

9567 Aircraft International Charters,
        Inc.
      Designer: Joanne T. West

9568 Curtis Air Freight, Inc.
      Designer: Joanne T. West

9569 Wah Wee
      Designer: Joanne T. West

9570 The Courtyard
      Designer: Joanne T. West

9571 The Dallace Palace
      Designer: Joanne T. West

9572 Granny's Attic
      Designer: Joanne T. West

9573 R.G. Maxwell's
      Designer: Joanne T. West

9574 Dallas-Ft. Worth Polo Club
      Designer: Joanne T. West

9575

9579

9576

9580

9577

9581

9578

9582

9583

9584

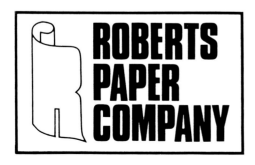

9585

9575   Our Town
        Designer: Joanne T. West

9576   Share In Success
        Designer: Joanne T. West

9577   Professional Connections
        Designer: Joanne T. West

9578   La Miranda Cancun
        Designer: Joanne T. West

9579   Weber-Hall, Inc.
        Designer: Joanne T. West

9580   Union Bank & Trust
        Designer: Joanne T. West

9581   Johnson Financial Services, Inc.
        Designer: Joanne T. West

9582   The Kerens Bank
        Designer: Joanne T. West

9583   Tucker, Johnson & Smelzer, Inc.
        Designer: Joanne T. West

9584   Mahoney Real Estate
        Designer: Joanne T. West

9585   Roberts Paper Company
        Designer: Joanne T. West

9586

HOMESTEAD
REAL·ESTATE

9590

9587

HAY MASTER

9591

9588

9592

9589

9593

9594

9595

9596

9597

9597   Star Channel, Warner Comm.
Designer: Alan Peckolick

9598

9599

9597   Star Channel, Warner Comm.
         Designer: Alan Peckolick

9598   Il Troia Restaurant
         Designer: Andy Engel

9599   Le Cou Cou Restaurant
         Designer: Bill Murphy

9600   Croissant's USA
         Designer: Bill Murphy

9600

9601

9605

9602

9606

9603

9607

9604

9608

9609

SHERWOOD PRODUCTIONS

9610

9611

9612

HOLLYWOOD HUMAN SERVICES PROJECT

9616

9613

CINEFLEX PICTURES

9617

9614

SKIPSEY
INTERNATIONAL

9618

9615

THE CENTRUM

9619

9620

9621

9622

9612   Hollywood Human Services
Designer: Ken Anderson

9613   Cineflex Pictures Company
Designer: Hoi Ping Law

9614   Skipsey Race Team
Designer: Hoi Ping Law

9615   The Centrum Commercial Bldg.
Designer: Alexander Pearman

9616   Applause Records
Designer: Rod Dyer

9617   Paramount Pictures
Designer: Rod Dyer

9618   Gaylord Productions
Designer: Bill Murphy

9619   Hotline Sports Boutique
Designer: Bill Tom

9620   XETI Records
Designer: Rod Dyer

9621   Elegence Magazine
Designer: Bill Murphy

9622   Oublier, Inc.
Designer: Hoi Ping Law

9623

9627

JACKSON PRODUCTIONS LTD

9624

9628

CAROLCO

9625

9629

RETINA FILMS

9626

PREMIERE ™

9630

BEVERLY CENTER

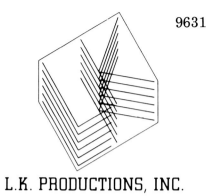

9631

L.K. PRODUCTIONS, INC.

9632

9633

9623	Origao Fashions Designer: Rod Dyer
9624	Frank & Christine Zane Designer: Bill Tom
9625	SelecTV Subscription TV Designer: Hoi Ping Law
9626	Premiere Designer: Rod Dyer
9627	Jackson Productions, Ltd. Designer: Ken Anderson
9628	Carolco Designer: Rod Dyer
9629	Retina Films Designer: Bill Tom
9630	Beckett Investment Corporation Designer: Hoi Ping Law
9631	L.K. Productions Designer: Bill Tom
9632	Future Flash Designer: Bill Murphy
9633	One Publishing, Inc. Designer: Rod Dyer

9634

9638

9635

TreScalini

9639

PISTOL PRODUCTIONS

9636

METAMORPHOSES

9640

WILSHIRE HOUSE

9637

First National Bank of Beverly Hills

9641

MARCO POLO

9642

9643

9644

9645

9649

9646

9650

9647

9651

9648

9652

9653

9654

9655

9656

9660

9657

9661

9658

9662

9659

9663

9664

9656	L'Eclair Restaurant Designer: Bill Murphy
9657	PG's Fast & Natural Designer: Bill Murphy
9658	Jones Intercable, Inc. Designer: Andy Engel
9659	Embassy Pictures Designer: Andy Engel
9660	Ira Teller & Company Designer: Andy Engel
9661	Universal Pictures Designer: Andy Engel

9665

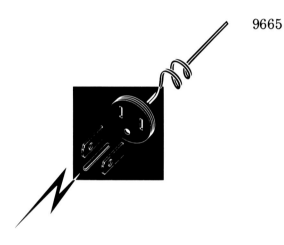

9662	Paramount Pictures Designer: Andy Engel
9663	Bank of Los Angeles Designer: Hoi Ping Law
9664	Drake-Chenault Designer: Andy Engel
9665	Zeon, Ltd. Designer: Bill Tom
9666	Paramount Television Designer: Hoi Ping Law

9666

9667

9671

PACIFIC ELECTRIC PICTURES

9668

9672

Patti's Productions

9669

Foundation For
America's Sexually Exploited Children, Inc.

9673

MOTOWN PRODUCTIONS

9670

PAVILLION
COMMUNICATIONS

9674

THE DISNEY CHANNEL

CATPEOPLE 9675

 9676

 9677

9678

SelecTV

9682

Coffee Company

9679

PURSUIT

9683

Candy Co

9680

FOTONOVEL

9684

.JAMES.
Kitchen
BEARD'S

9681

THE SWEATSHOP TUFF STUFF

9685

ARTWORK

9686

9687

9688

J. Westfahl 9689

SUMMER BEND 9693

9690

WILD BASIN
ATRIUM
OFFICE · PARK
9694

RAMSGATE FARM 9691

GORDON 9695

BAYLOR UNIVERSITY
CHARTERED BY THE REPUBLIC OF TEXAS
Centennial at Waco
1845 · INDEPENDENCE · 1886 · WACO · 1986
9692

BUBBA'S ROADHOUSE 9696

9697

9689 (Proposal) J. Westfahl
      Designer: Charlotte Potts

9690 The Counselors
      Designer: Charlotte Potts

9691 Baylor University
      Designer: Charlotte Potts

9692 Ramsgate Farm
      Designer: Charlotte Potts

9698

9693 Summer's Properties
      Designer: Jim Gordon

9694 Wild-Basin Atrium Park Assn.
      Designer: Jim Gordon

9695 Self Promotion
      Designer: Jim Gordon

9696 Grinnell, Kucnel, Martinez Partners
      Designer: Jim Gordon

9697 Cimarron Properties (Proposed)
      Designer: Jim Gordon

9698 Ira Yates
      Designer: Jim Gordon

9699

9699 Hawkeye's Restaurant
      Designer: Jim Gordon

9700

9704

9701

9705

9702

9706

9703

9707

9708

9709

9710

9700	Cimarron Properties Designer: Jim Gordon
9701	Walter Carrington Designer: Jim Gordon
9702	The Mews Designer: Jim Gordon
9703	Gordon and Gallagher Designer: Jim Gordon
9704	Stan Davis, Developer Designer: Jim Gordon
9705	Rubicon Publishing Designer: Jim Gordon
9706	Woerner Properties Designer: Jim Gordon
9707	Rick Hardin, Developer Designer: Jim Gordon
9708	Little League Baseball Designer: Jim Gordon
9709	Weingarten Realty Designer: Jim Gordon
9710	Sally Grinnell Designer: Jim Gordon

9711

9715

9712

9716

9713

9717

9714

9718

9719

9720

9721

9722

NORTH AUSTIN SAVINGS

9726

9723

9727

9724

9728

9725

9729

9730

EXECUTIVE BANC

9731

9732

9733

9737

9734

9738

9735

9739

9736

9740

9741

9742

9743

9733   Janice Kay, Hairstylist
        Designer: Jim Gordon

9734   Woerner Properties
        Designer: Jim Gordon

9735   Walter Carrington
        Designer: Jim Gordon

9736   Gonzalo Barrientos
        Designer: Jim Gordon

9737   Self Promotion
        Designer: Jim Gordon

9738   Unicorn Construction Company
        Designer: Jim Gordon

9739   The Market Place
        Designer: Jim Gordon

9740   Thompson Properties
        Designer: Jim Gordon

9741   In Depth Research, Investigative
          Services
        Designer: Jim Gordon

9742   Summers Properties
        Designer: Jim Gordon

9743   Cimarron Properties
        Designer: Jim Gordon

9744

9748

9745

WESTLAKE

9749

9746

9750

National
Communications

9747

9751

9752

9753

9754

9744   Bettie Gordon
Designer: Jim Gordon

9745   Westlake Management Company
Designer: Jim Gordon

9746   Fields Group
Designer: Jim Gordon

9747   Tom Allen's Barbeque
Designer: Jim Gordon

9748   Home Management
Designer: Jim Gordon

9749   Harren Financial Group
Designer: Jim Gordon

9750   National Communications
Designer: Jim Gordon

9751   Self Promotion
Designer: Jim Gordon

9752   Gill Company
Designer: Jim Gordon

9753   R.D. Borkoski Graphics
Designer: Bob Borkoski

9754   Mast Headasthead For 24 Karat
Designer: Bob Borkoski

9755

9759

9756

9760

9757

9761

9758

9762

9763

9764

CIQROO

9765

Plaza Montesinos

9755	Mast Head For Newsletter Matthews Int'l Corp. Designer: Bob Borkoski
9756	Mast Head For Newsletter Matthews Int'l Corp. Designer: Bob Borkoski
9757	Keystone Organ & Piano Designer: Bob Borkoski
9758	Robinson/Ogilvy Designer: Bob Borkoski
9759	Matthews Int'l Corp. Designer: Bob Borkoski
9760	Matthews Int'l Corp. Designer: Bob Borkoski
9761	Trident Underwater Club Designer: Bob Borkoski
9762	Trident Underwater Club Designer: Bob Borkoski
9763	Mount Rose Cemetery Designer: Bob Borkoski
9764	Ciqroo Designer: Allen Miller
9765	Museu Montesinos Designer: Allen Miller

9766

9770

9767

9771

9768

9772

9769

9773

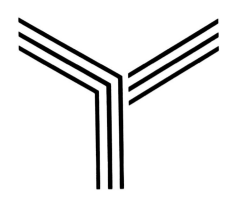

9774

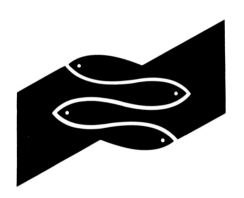

9775

9776

9766   Scotty's Cookies
Designer: Allen Miller

9767   Prinza
Designer: Allen Miller

9768   Flight Trails
Designer: Allen Miller

9769   California Rainbow
Designer: Allen Miller

9770   Ramos Y. Asociados
Designer: Allen Miller

9771   Charlotte Jenson
Designer: Allen Miller

9772   Ciqroo
Designer: Allen Miller

9773   Bristol Bay
Designer: Allen Miller

9774   William Birman Company
Designer: Allen Miller

9775   Pesquera Santa Ursula
Designer: Allen Miller

9776   California Indoor Soccer Academy
Designer: Allen Miller

9777

9781

THE BEACON

9778

9782

SUTUN

9779

9783

9780

9784

9785

9786

Community Bank

HONDO, TEXAS · Member FDIC

9787

9777	Corporacion Consultora	Designer: Allen Miller
9778	Advanced Airport Equipment	Designer: Allen Miller
9779	Suites Meza Del Mar	Designer: Allen Miller
9780	Girls Soccer Organization	Designer: Allen Miller
9781	The Beacon	Designer: Allen Miller
9782	Sutun	Designer: Allen Miller
9783	Pacific Soap Company	Designer: Allen Miller
9784	Capricorn Energy	Designer: Kim Paxson
9785	Landmark Graphics	Designer: Jon Bader
9786	Delta Feeders Inc.	Designer: Jon Bader
9787	Community National Bank	Designer: Jon Bader

9892

9896

9893

9897

delaware
energy
extension
service

9894

L.E. MINNS

9898

9895

CORK LTD

9899

9900

9901

9902

9903

9892	Silverbird Film Production Designer: Southam Associates, Inc.
9893	SSS Gears Co. of England Designer: Southam Associates, Inc.
9894	State of Delaware Designer: Southam Associates, Inc.
9895	Atlantic Aviation Designer: Southam Associates, Inc.
9896	Helcon Concrete Contractor Designer: Southam Associates, Inc.
9897	E.I. du Pont de Nemours & Co., Inc. Designer: Southam Associates, Inc.
9898	L.E. Minns Heating & Alc. Designer: Southam Associates, Inc.
9899	Cork, Ltd. General Contractors Designer: Southam Associates, Inc.
9900	Computer Hows Software Systems Designer: Southam Associates, Inc.
9901	Stat Stat Designer: Southam Associates, Inc.
9902	Phalco, Inc. Designer: Southam Associates, Inc.
9903	Delaware Theater Company Designer: Southam Associates, Inc.

9904

T·I·D·E

For ETHYLENE COPOLYMERS

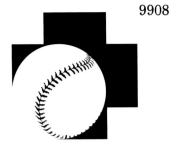

9908

Professional
Baseball
Athletic Trainers
Society

9905

Strategic Deployment of Resources

9909

9910

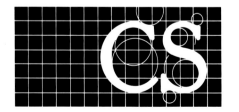

9906

9907

9911

 9912

 9913

9914

 9915

9904	E.I. du Pont de Nemours & Co., Inc. Designer: Southam Associates, Inc.
9905	E.I. du Pont de Nemours & Co., Inc. Designer: Southam Associates, Inc.
9906	Davis Studio Designer: Southam Associates, Inc.
9907	City Systems, Inc. Designer: Southam Associates, Inc.
9908	Professional Baseball Athletic Trainers Society Designer: Southam Assocs., Inc.
9909	Wilmington Travel Services, Inc. Designer: Southam Assocs., Inc.
9910	State of Delaware Bicentennial Film Designer: Dale Southam
9911	American Textile Products Designer: Dale Southam
9912	The Alley Designer: Dale Southam
9913	Wilmington Vietnam Veterans Leadership Program, Inc. Designer: Southam Assocs., Inc.
9914	Brandy Wine Memorial Service Designer: Southam Assocs., Inc.
9915	Avery's (Sheraton) Bar & Lounge Designer: Dale Southam

9916

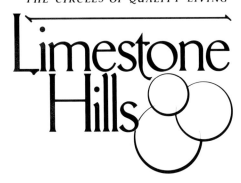

9920

9917

THE CIRCLES OF QUALITY LIVING

9921

9918

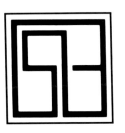

9922

9919

9923

9924

9925

9926

9927

9916   Univ. of Delaware ('79)
        Designer: Dale Southam

9917   Gilpin Realtors
        Designer: Southam Assocs., Inc.

9918   Healy Management Services
        Designer: Southam Assocs., Inc.

9919   G.S. Booth & Company
        Designer: Southam Assocs., Inc.

9920   Alcann Projects, Inc.
        Designer: Soileau Studio

9921   No-Whar but Texas Club
        Designer: Soileau Studio

9922   Bi-M Instruments, Inc.
        Designer: Soileau Studio

9923   Jan Norris Adv. & P.R., Inc.
        Designer: Soileau Studio

9924   Melangs
        Designer: Soileau Studio

9925   Soileau Studio
        Designer: Soileau Studio

9926   Les McDonald Adv., Inc.
        Designer: Loileau Studio

9927   Houstons Wild West Club
        Designer: Soileau Studio

9928

Continental
RADIO COMPANY, INC.

9932

9929

9933

LOVE PLATES

9930

SECURITY WORLD

9934

Marlin
Drilling Co.,
Inc.

9931

WOODWAY
LOCATORS

9935

CREATIVE VENTURES

9936

9937

9938

9939

9928   Continental Radio Co., Inc.
Designer: Soileau Studio

9929   KULF 790
Designer: Soileau Studio

9930   Security World
Designer: Soileau Studio

9931   Woodway Locators
Designer: Soileau Studio

9932   Industrial Advertising
Designer: Soileau Studio

9933   China Portrait Systems
Designer: Soileau Studio

9934   Marlin Drilling Co. Inc.
Designer: Soileau Studio

9935   Creative Ventures
Designer: Soileau Studio

9936   Joes Record Rack
Designer: Soileau Studio

9937   Creative Media Services, Inc.
Designer: Soileau Studio

9938   Sunset Enterprises
Designer: Soileau Studio

9939   En Hoc Ltd.
Designer: Soileau Studio

9940

9944

9941

9945

9942

9946

9943

9947

9948

9949

9950

9951

9940	Syconex
	Designer: Soileau Studio
9941	Vacuum Systems, Inc.
	Designer: Soileau Studio
9942	Team Inc.
	Designer: Soileau Studio
9943	Dunn Welding Equip. Co. Inc.
	Designer: Soileau Studio
9944	WKB International
	Designer: Soileau Studio
9945	Control Systems
	Designer: Soileau Studio
9946	Concordia Inc.
	Designer: Soileau Studio
9947	IV-L, Inc./Lincoln Comm., Inc./ Hotel, Inc.
	Designer: Soileau Studio
9948	Relocation Services of Services of Houston
	Designer: Soileau Studio
9949	Small Talk Children's Shop
	Designer: Soileau Studio
9950	New Braunfels Armadillo Assoc.
	Designer: Soileau Studio
9951	A&W International Couriers
	Designer: Soileau Studio

9952

9956

9953

9957

9954

9958

9955

9959

9960

AVPAC CORPORATION

CORPORATE
AMERICA
APARTMENT SUITES

9961

9952   Whiting Oilfield Rental Inc.
        Designer: Soileau Studio

9953   Atlas Fluid Controls Corp.
        Designer: Soileau Studio

9954   Environmental Control Products,
          Inc.
        Designer: Soileau Studio

9955   Theatre Showcase
        Designer:Soileau Studio

9956   Michael Hart Photography
        Designer: Soileau Studio

9957   Deyo Fawcett
        Designer: Soileau Studio

9958   National Panel Systems, Inc.
        Designer: Soileau Studio

9959   Marketing Ideas of Texas, Inc.
        Designer: Soileau Studio

9960   AVPAC Corporation
        Designer: Soileau Studio

9961   Corporate America Apartment
          Suites
        Designer: Soileau Studio

9962   National Assn. of Women in
          Commerical Real Estate
        Designer: Soileau Studio

9962

NATIONAL ASSOCIATION OF WOMEN
IN COMMERCIAL REAL ESTATE

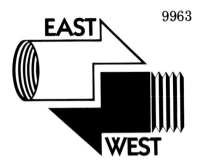

9963

9967

Coffey
Russey
& Assoc., Inc.

9964

Lafayette West

9968

BETHANY
INTERNATIONAL INC.

9965

APPLIED
COMBUSTION
SYSTEMS, INC.

9969

The specialists

9966

BEW

9970

instrumatics
INCORPORATED

9971

9972

9973

9974

ORTHOPEDIC & SPORTS MEDICINE
CLINIC ASSOCIATION

9963   East West Trading Co., Inc./
       East West Pipe Threaders, Inc.
      Designer: Soileau Studio

9964   Lafayette West
      Designer: Soileau Studio

9965   Applied Combustion Sys., Inc.
      Designer: Soileau Studio

9966   Boone & Wright
      Designer: Soileau Studio

9967   Coffey Russey & Assoc., Inc.
      Designer: Soileau Studio

9968   Natl. Pane
      Designer: Soileau Studio

9969   The Specialists
      Designer: Soileau Studio

9970   Instrumentics Inc.
      Designer: Soileau Studio

9971   Liz Grimes
      Designer: Catherine Carrier

9972   J. Lee Douglas Familty Dentistry,
      Nashville
      Designer: Catherine Carrier

9973   Crosswinds Horns, Atlanta
      Designer: Catherine Carrier

9974   Orthopedic & Sports Medicine
      Clinic Assn.
      Designer: Catherine Carrier

9975

9979

9976

9980

9977

9981

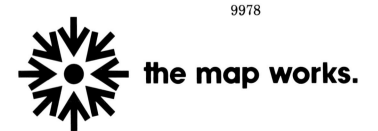

9978

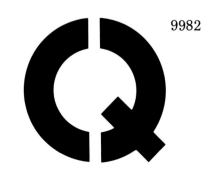

9982

9983

9984

9975	Fox Artist Management, Nashville Designer: Catherine Carrier
9976	Lay Renewal Ministries, St. Louis Designer: Catherine Carrier
9977	S. Hunter Gordon (Cartographer) Designer: S. Hunter Gordon
9978	The Map Works Designer: S. Hunter Gordon
9979	Keepers of The Light Designer: Tom Yasuda
9980	Cardinal Investments Internatl. Designer: Tom Yasuda
9981	Military Graphics Designer: Tom Yasuda
9982	C.Q. Enterprises Designer: Tom Yasuda
9983	West Central Assn. Designer: Visual Design Center, Inc.
9984	Mortgage Guaranty Ins. Corp. Designer: Visual Design Center, Inc.
9985	ICOR International Inc. Designer: Visual Design Center, Inc.

9985

9986

9990

9987

GEMET inc.

9991

9988

9992

9989

9993

Ames ISU Tennis Club 9994

9995

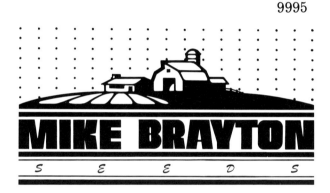

9996

Career Counseling

9986   First Natl. Bank of Leesport
(Proposed)
Designer: David Bullock

9987   Gemet, Inc.
Designer: David Bullock

9988   Clauser Office Supplies
Designer: David Bullock

9989   First Natl. Bank of Leesport
Designer: David Bullock

9990   First Natl. Bank of Leesport
(Proposed)
Designer: David Bullock

9991   Papillion, Imports, Commerce,
Distribution
Designer: David Bullock

9992   Ames Society of Furniture
Designer: Mickelson Design &
Associates

9993   Airline Luggage Service
Designer: Alan Mickelson

9994   Ames ISU Tennis Club
Designer: Mickelson Design &
Associates

9995   Mike Brayton Seeds, Inc.
Designer: Mickelson Design &
Associates

9996   Career Counseling
Designer: Mickelson Design &
Associates

9997

EXPLORER

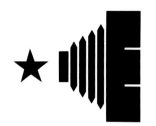

10001

9998

10002

DOMUS

9999

THE FENCING CENTER

10003

Big Sur

10000

Fish again & pasta too!

10004

OLD TOWN
·LOS GATOS·CALIFORNIA·

...Where the mountains meet the marketplace!

10005

10006

GET THE FLAVOR OF

HAWAII

UNITED AIRLINES

10007

10008

10012

10009

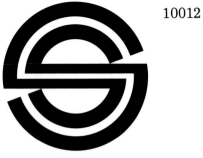

10013

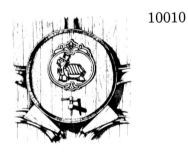

10010

10014

10015

10011

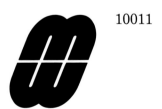

10016

Vacation Values

10017

10018

10019

Health Education Television Network

10008	Town of Los Gatos	Designer: Rick Tharp Did It
10009	Dimension in Health, Massage Therapy	Designer: Rick Tharp Did It
10010	Velvet Turtle Restaurants	Designer: Rick Tharp Did It
10011	Marion Wheeler Interiors	Designer: Rick Tharp Did It
10012	Orthodontic Services, Inc.	Designer: Don Borger
10013	Regis Industrial Supply	Designer: Don Borger
10014	SDI Inc.	Designer: Don Borger
10015	Westlake Metal Industries	Designer: Don Borger
10016	Vacation Vallies	Designer: Don Borger
10017	Bavarian Village	Designer: Don Borger/Ken Liska
10018	Kavco Materials, Inc.	Designer: Ken Liska
10019	Greater Cleveland Hosp. Assn.	Designer: Don Borger

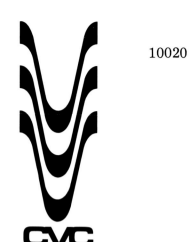

10020

CVC

10021

10024

Alloy
Molded Products, Inc.

10025

10022

10026

LUTHERAN
HIGH
SCHOOL
WEST

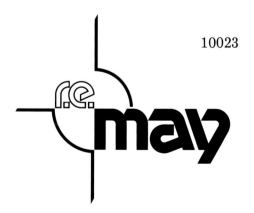

10023

10027

10028

10029

10030

10031

10020	Cleveland Vibrator Company Designer: Don Borger
10021	Design Associates Designer: Ken Liska
10022	Bay Heating & Air Conditioning Designer: Don Borger
10023	R.E. May Designer: Don Borger
10024	Alloy Molded Products Designer: Don Borger
10025	Patrick's Designer: Ken Liska
10026	Lutheran High School West Designer: Don Borger
10027	Robert J. Claypool Agency Designer: Patti Russo
10028	T&T Delivery Designer: Patti Russo
10029	Patti Russo/P.J. Graphics Designer: Patti Russo/ Ed Saunders
10030	Travel Time Inc. Designer: Patti Russo
10031	P. Computers Designer: Patti Russo/ Ed Saunders

10032

10036

10033

10037

KAATERSKILL ANIMAL LEAGUE

10034

10038

10035

10039

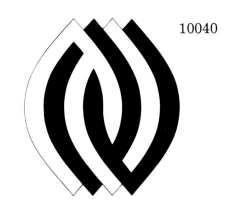

10040

10032   A-Z Plantery
        Designer: Patti Russo

10041

10033   Medworld Inc.
        Designer: Patti Russo/
          Ed Saunders

10034   Soft Print
        Designer: Mickelson Design &
          Associates

10035   Distribution Sales & Svs. Div.
        Designer: Kevin L. Hall

10036   Five-Mile Birthday Run
        Designer: Kevin L. Hall

10037   Karterskill Animal League
        Designer: Kevin L. Hall

10042

10038   A Coffee Company
        Designer: Kevin L. Hall

10039   The Jos. Garneau Company
        Designer: Gianninoto Assocs.

10040   Batus Inc.
        Designer: Gianninoto Assocs.

10041   Plumrose
        Designer: Gianninoto Assocs.

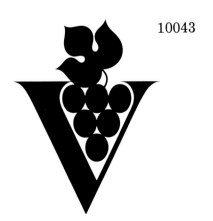

10043

10042   Hipp Werke KG
        Designer: Gianninoto Assocs.

10043   Vinicola Vergel SA
        Designer: Gianninoto Assocs.

10044

10048

Frutas Mundet, S.A.

Jugos De

10045

10049

IN VITRO FERTILIZATION

STRASSEL'S ™

10046

CLEANUP CREW

10050

Sports

MEDICINE

10047

10051

10052

10053

10054

10044	Dak Foods, Inc. Designer: Gianninoto Assocs.
10045	Jugos de Fruitas Mundet Designer: Gianninoto Assocs.
10046	H.P. Hood, Inc. Designer: Gianninoto Assocs.
10047	Health West Designer: Diane Kuntz
10048	The Homer C. Pleasent Spine Institute Designer: Diane Kuntz
10049	Northridge Hosp. Medical Ctr. Designer: Diane Kuntz
10050	The Cleanup Crew Designer: Lauren Smith
10051	Love Notes Greeting Cards Designer: Lauren Smith
10052	Budget Print Centers Designer: Lauren Smith
10053	Fine Australian Opal & Colored Gemstones Designer: Nash Hernandez
10054	Emergency Care Center Designer: Nash Hernandez

10055

10059

10056

10060

10057

10061

10058

10062

Bronson
METHODIST HOSPITAL

10063

InterAct

10064

JANET WINTERS
REALTY

10065

10055   Wind Song
        Designer: Gene Ten Brick Design

10056   Ken Keller Productions
        Designer: Gene Ten Brick Design

10057   Columbus U.S.A. Assoc.
        Designer: Gene Ten Brick Design

10058   Sellers Marketing Services
        Designer: Gene Ten Brick Design

10059   Gene Ten Brick
        Designer: Gene Ten Brick Design

10060   Eagle Freight System Inc.
        Designer: Gene Ten Brick Design

10061   Shrine Circus
        Designer: Gene Ten Brick Design

10062   Bronson Methodist Hospital
        Designer: Gene Ten Brick Design

10063   InterAct (Hoover)
        Designer: Gene Ten Brick Design

10064   Janet Winters Realty
        Designer: Alexander Bridge

10065   Gage Molding
        Designer: Alexander Bridge

10066

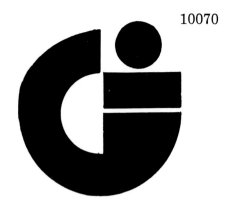

10070

10067

SHAPE TAPE AUTOMATION

10071

ATAVAR CORPORATION

10068

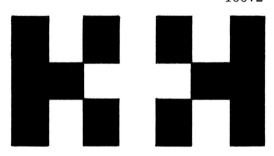

10072

10069

10073

10074

10075

10076

10077

MOORE BUSINESS SYSTEMS INC.

10066   Vortech Corporation
Designer: Alexander Bridge

10067   Shape Tape Automation
Designer: Alexander Bridge

10068   Avatar Corporation
Designer: Alexander Bridge

10069   L.A. Water Treatment Co.
Designer: Courtland Thomas
White

10070   Genesis International, Ltd.
Designer: Courtland Thomas
White

10071   J.J. Fleck, Inc.
Designer: Courtland Thomas
White

10072   Haywood & Haywood Assocs.
Designer: Courtland Thomas
White

10073   KUER Radio (NPR Affiliate)
Designer: Scott Engen

10074   PSA
Designer: Beth Maryon

10075   College of Law, Univ. of Utah
Designer: Scott Engen &
Beth Maryon

10076   Internatl. Medical Tech., Corp.
Designer: Aucella & Assocs., Inc.

10077   Moore Business Systems, Inc.
Designer: Aucella & Assocs., Inc.

10078

10082

10079

10083

10080

10084

10081

10085

10086

10087

10088

10089

10090

10094

GRAPH
INK
STUDIOS

10091

.M GREENE

10095

COLLAGE

10092

The DEP**ART**MENT

10096

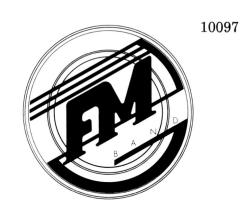

PB-KBB Inc.

10093

10097

10098

SYSTEMATIC MANAGEMENT SERVICES

10099

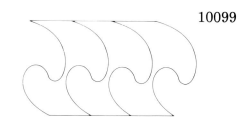

T I D E S
T O W N H O M E S

10100

10090	DUCI Designer: Carlos M. Segura
10091	Graph Ink Studios Designer: Carlos M. Segura
10092	Collage Record Sales Designer: Carlos M. Segura
10093	PB/KBB Inc. Designer: Carlos M. Segura
10094	DUCI Designer: Carlos M. Segura
10095	Michael Greene Designer: Carlos M. Segura
10096	DUCI Designer: Carlos M. Segura
10097	FM Musical Group Designer: Carlos M. Segura
10098	Systematic Management Svs. Designer: Carlos M. Segura
10099	Tides Townhomes Designer: Carlos M. Segura
10100	Sundown Theatre Designer: Carlos M. Segura
10101	Carlos M. Segura Designer: Carlos M. Segura

10101

10102

10106

10103

10107

10104

10108

10105

10109

10110

10111

10112

10113

10102   J.D. Studios
Designer: Jim Dildine

10103   Bayshore Gardens
Designer: Jim Dildine

10104   Tal Inc.
Designer: Jim Dildine

10105   Image Ink, Co.
Designer: Jim Dildine

10106   Stone Mtn. Condominiums
Designer: Tielemans/Lee

10107   Entrepreneurs Exchange
Designer: Tielemans/Lee

10108   Home Sports Unlimited
Designer: Tielemans/Lee

10109   Knut & Clydes Saloon
Designer: Tielemans/Lee

10110   Nostalgia Ice Cream & Sandwiches
Designer: Tielemans/Lee

10111   Quail Creek R.V. Park
Designer: Tielemans/Lee

10112   Shanley's Restaurant
Designer: Tielemans/Lee

10113   Dixie Downs R.V. Resort
Designer: Tielemans/Lee

10114

10118

10115

10119

10116

10120

10117

10121

10122

10123

10124

10125

10114   Nielson's Frozen Custard
Designer: Tielemans/Lee

10115   Spilker Construction
Designer: Tielemans/Lee

10116   Willow Run Resort
Condominiums
Designer: Tielemans/Lee

10117   Big Shot
Designer: Tielemans/Lee

10118   Sun West Resorts Inc.
Designer: Tielemans/Lee

10119   Pizzazz Pizza
Designer: Tielemans/Lee

10120   Sun Time Tours
Designer: Tielemans/Lee

10121   W.G. Clarke
Designer: Jay Gold

10122   W.G. Clarke
Designer: Jay Gold

10123   Individual Learning Systems
Designer: Scott Engen/
James S. Omar

10124   Washington Commons
Designer: Hans Boye Boyeson/
Robert Flanagan

10125   Jackson Homes
Designer: Ken Ginn/Houston

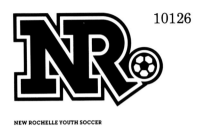

10126

NEW ROCHELLE YOUTH SOCCER

10130

PURCHASE PARK

10127

THE HOME INSURANCE COMPANY

10131

W I N G S

10128

ART GALLERY/21 SOUTH MOGER AVE./MT KISCO NY (914) 666-6064

10132

10129

NATIONAL CAPTIONING INSTITUTE, INC.

10133

PARK AVENUE PLAZA

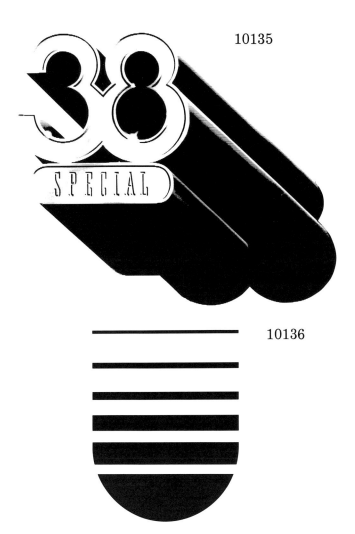

10135

10136

10137

Columbia Pictures

10141

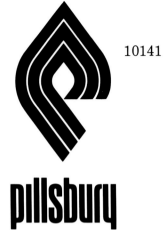

pillsbury

10138

10142

10139

10143

10140

Scholastic Productions

10144

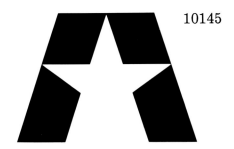

10145

the american federation of arts

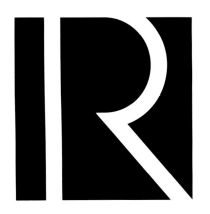

10146

10147

10148

GENERAL FELT INDUSTRIES

10137   Columbia Pictures
        Designer: Philip Gips

10138   QUBE
        Designer: Gips/Balkind & Assocs.

10139   New York Fire House
        Designer: Philip Gips

10140   Scholastic Productions
        Designer: Philip Gips

10141   Pillsbury
        Designer: Philip Gips

10142   Del Ray Books
        Designer: Diana Graham

10143   Ramco
        Designer: Diana Graham

10144   American Broadcasting Co.
        Designer: Diana Graham

10145   The American Federation of Arts
        Designer: Philip Gips

10146   L.F. Rothschild Co.
        Designer: Philip Gips/
          Diana Graham

10147   The Clean Community System
        Designer: Diana Graham

10148   General Felt Industries
        Designer: Philip Gips

10149

10153

10150

10154

10151

10155

10152

10156

10157

10158

10159

10149   Angelo Brothers
Designer: Kerry Polite

10150   Ransome Airlines
Designer: Marci Mansfield-Fickes

10151   Warehouse Imports
Designer: Marci Mansfield-Fickes

10152   Warehouse Imports
Designer: Kerry Polite

10153   Angelo Brothers
Designer: Kerry Polite

10154   Giles and Ransome
Designer: Kerry Polite

10155   Bon Giorno Cappucino
Designer: Marci Mansfield-Fickes

10156   Wallace Furnitire
Designer: Kerry Polite

10157   Community Light & Sound
Designer: Kerry Polite

10158   Holiday Inn
Designer: Bill Middleton

10159   Warehouse Imports
Designer: Marci Mansfield-Ficke

IN STYLE!

10160

10164

10161

10165

10162

10166

9&b

10163

10167

 10168

10169

PROFIT MARGIN

10170

THE BREWERY
TOWNHOUSES

SYSTEM **2000** 10171

10172

10176

10173

10177

10174

10178

10175

10179

10180

10181

10182

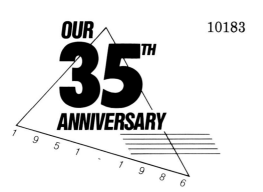

10183

10172   Angelo/Osram
         Designer: Marci Mansfield-Ficke

10173   Wallace Furniture
         Designer: Marci Mansfield-Ficke

10174   Ransome Engine Power
         Designer: Peter Sasgen

10175   Si and Patsy Mansfield
         Designer: Marci Mansfield-Ficke

10176   Angelo Brothers
         Designer: Kerry Polite

10177   Country Workshops
         Designer: Kerry Polite

10178   Atlas
         Designer: Marci Mansfield-Fickes

10179   Wallace Office
         Designer: Marci Mansfield-Fickes

10180   Continental Imports
         Designer: Marci Mansfield-Fickes

10181   Angelo Brothers
         Designer: Bill Middleton

10182   Weathervane Farms
         Designer: Marci Mansfield-Fickes

10183   Warehouse Imports
         Designer: Bill Middleton

10184

Landon
Middle
School

10188

10185

graftronix

10189

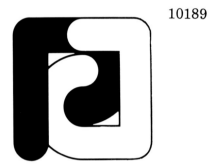

10186

10190

10187

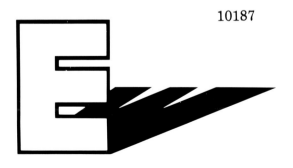

10191

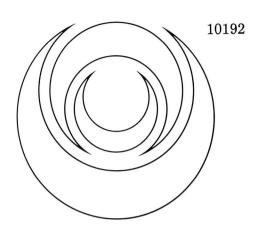

10192

10193

10194

10195

10184   Landon Middle School
Designer: Myle J. Scrinopskie

10185   Graftronix, Inc.
Designer: Paul Pullara

10186   Divspec (Diversifed Specialties, Inc.)
Designer: Paul Pullara

10187   Edwards & West, Inc.
Designer: Paul Pullara

10188   Reliable Threaded Products, Inc.
Designer: Paul Pullara

10189   Program Automation, Inc.
Designer: Paul Pullara

10190   Audio Independents, Inc.
Designer: Brian Flahive/
Julia Lee Prospero

10191   Vini Vidi Video
Designer: Brian Flahive

10192   Uttara Dances
Designer: Brian Flahive

10193   American Assn. of Physician's Assistants
Designer: Brian Flahive

10194   Ear Food, Electronic Music
Designer: Brian Flahive

10195   Ergo Corporation
Designer: Brian Flahive

10196

10200

10197

10201

10198

10202

10199

10203

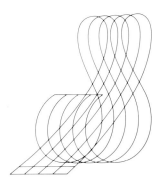

10204

10205

10206

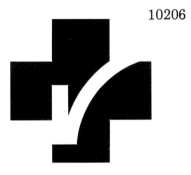

10207

10196   The Airworks Group
Designer: Brian Flahive/
Julia Lee Prospero

10197   Time Machine
Designer: Brian Flahive

10198   Ear Food, Electronic Music
Designer: Brian Flahive

10199   JEL Electronic Music
Designer: Brian Flahive

10200   Bynamics Inc.
Designer: Brian Flahive/
Julia Lee Prospero

10201   ITM International SA
Designer: Pentagram Design Ltd.

10202   Science Management Corp.
Designer: Pentagram Design, Ltd.

10203   New Britain Symphony Society
Designer: Pentagram Design, Ltd.

10204   CorpAir
Designer: Pentagram Design, Ltd.

10205   Hyspan Precision Products, Inc.
Designer: Susan Merritt

10206   MedSource International
Designer: Michael Whalen

10207   MediChek
Designer: Michael Whalen

10208

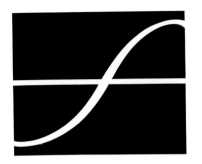

10212

10209

10213

10210

10214

10211

10215

10216

10217

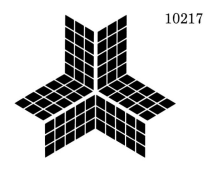

10218

10219

10208   Fry & Stone Assocs. ASLA
        Designer: Michael Whalen

10209   San Diego Eye Institute
        Designer: Michael Whalen

10210   Flambeau Paper Corp.
        Designer: Russ Mueller/
          Jerry Slaasted

10211   California Mart Shoe Market
        Designer: Eugene Cheltenham

10212   Skatey's
        Designer: Eugene Cheltenham

10213   Gerson's
        Designer: Eugene Cheltenham

10214   Sun King Publishing Group
        Designer: Eugene Cheltenham

10215   Tom Thornburg
        Designer: Max McDonald

10216   Grand Central Racquetball Club
        Designer: Zahor Design Inc.

10217   Natl. Assn. of Bus. Economists
        Designer: Paul Ison/
          Patrick Soo Hoo

10218   Naugles, Inc.
        Designer: Paul Ison

10219   Sonic
        Designer: Stan Volinsky

10220

10224

10221

10225

10222

10226

10223

10227

10228

10229

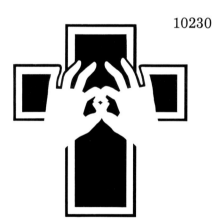

10230

10231

10232

10236

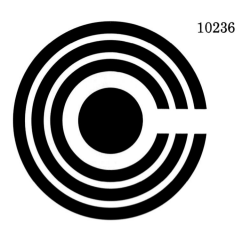

10233

10237

10234

GIIASH
COMMERCIAL PHOTOGRAPHY

10238

10235

10239

 10240

 10241

 10242

 10243

10232   Sign Language Interpreting
Accessibility
Designer: Ann Silver

10233   Mapet Ltd.-A Mayor Corp. Co.
Designer: Boaz Kimelman

10234   Gil Ash Commercial Photography
Designer: Soileau Studio

10235   Timmons Enterprises, Inc.
Designer: Richard A. Servatious

10236   HSI Management, Inc.
Designer: Richard A. Servatious

10237   Avondale Swim & Tennis Club
Designer: Don Connelly & Assocs.

10238   Independent Ins. Agents of GA
Designer: Don Connelly & Assocs.

10239   Sunbelt
Designer: Don Connelly & Assocs.

10240   Practitioner's Forum
Designer: Don Connelly & Assocs.

10241   Reconstruction Inc.
Designer: Don Connelly & Assocs.

10242   Betty's Tours
Designer: Don Connelly & Assocs.

10243   National Graphics
Designer: Don Connelly & Assocs.

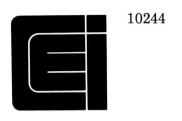

10244

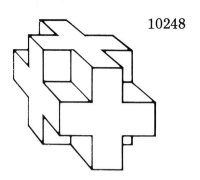

10248

10245

10249

10246

10250

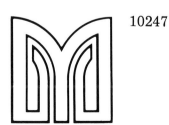

10247

10251

 10252

 10253

 10254

 10255

10244   Crusader Equipment Co.
        Designer: Don Connelly & Assocs.

10245   Bryant Electronics
        Designer: Don Connelly & Assocs.

10246   Organizational Development
        Designer: Don Connelly & Assocs.

10247   Moores Dept. Store (Proposed)
        Designer: Don Connelly & Assocs.

10248   Red Cross of Atlanta
        Designer: Don Connelly & Assocs.

10249   Bullard Realty
        Designer: Don Connelly & Assocs.

10250   New Market Business Park
        Designer: Don Connelly & Assocs.

10251   Grand Slam Golf Classic
        Designer: Don Connelly & Assocs.

10252   Creative Network Services
        Designer: Don Connelly & Assocs.

10253   Alvin Lee
        Designer: Don Connelly & Assocs.

10254   Hampton Green
        Designer: Don Connelly & Assocs.

10255   Newspaper In Education
        Designer: Don Connelly & Assocs.

10256

10260

10257

10261

10258

10262

10259

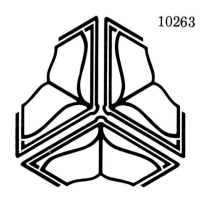

10263

 10264

 10265

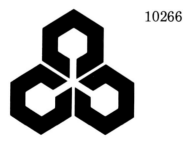 10266

 10267

10256 Metro Golf Tournament
Designer: Don Connelly & Assocs.

10257 Georgia Generals Soccer (Propos.)
Designer: Don Connelly & Assocs.

10258 Equity Investors of America
Designer: Don Connelly & Assocs.

10259 Don Connelly & Associates
Designer: Don Connelly & Assocs.

10260 Arthritis Foundation (Proposed)
Designer: Don Connelly & Assocs.

10261 The Country Store
Designer: Don Connelly & Assocs.

10262 The Selin Company
Designer: Don Connelly & Assocs.

10263 Commission of Continuing
Lawyer Competency (State
Board of Georgia
Designer: Don Connelly & Assocs.

10264 Big Heart Award
Designer: Don Connelly & Assocs.

10265 Electromagnetic Systems, Inc.
Designer: Don Connelly & Assocs.

10266 College Coaches Classic
Designer: Don Connelly & Assocs.

10267 Cotton States Classic (Proposed)
Designer: Don Connelly & Assocs.

10268

10272

10269

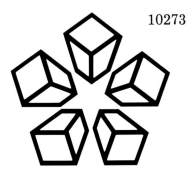

10273

10270

10274

10271

10275

10276

10277

10278

10279

10268	Condor Automotive	Designer: Don Connelly & Assocs.
10269	Avondale Community Action	Designer: Don Connelly & Assocs.
10270	T&B Scottdale Contractors	Designer: Don Connelly & Assocs.
10271	Speakers Forum	Designer: Don Connelly & Assocs.
10272	Mini-Tour Golf	Designer: Don Connelly & Assocs.
10273	Georgia Granite (Proposed)	Designer: Don Connelly & Assocs.
10274	Espirit Travel & Tours	Designer: Don Connelly & Assocs.
10275	Professional Assn. Management	Designer: Don Connelly & Assocs.
10276	Girafix Grafix	Designer: Don Connelly & Assocs.
10277	North American Newstime	Designer: Don Connelly & Assocs.
10278	Georgia Granite (Proposed)	Designer: Don Connelly & Assocs.
10279	Holder Well Company	Designer: Don Connelly & Assocs.

10280

10284

10281

10285

10282

10286

10283

10287

 10288

 10289

10290

10291

10280   Special Olympian
Designer: Don Connelly & Assocs.

10281   Associated Rubber Company
Designer: Don Connelly & Assocs.

10282   Hobis
Designer: Don Connelly & Assocs.

10283   Real Property Law Section
     (State Board of Georgia)
Designer: Don Connelly & Assocs.

10284   Sun Dynasty
Designer: Don Connelly & Assocs.

10285   Shaw & Parrott
Designer: Don Connelly & Assocs.

10286   TransAmerica
Designer: Don Connelly & Assocs.

10287   Automated Marketing
Designer: Don Connelly & Assocs.

10288   Chanley & Associates
Designer: Don Connelly & Assocs.

10289   Hampton Oaks
Designer: Don Connelly & Assocs.

10290   Specialty Graphics
Designer: Don Connelly & Assocs.

10291   Georgia Tax Conference
Designer: Don Connelly & Assocs.

 10292

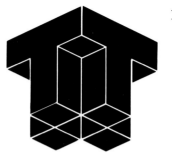 10296

 10293

 10297

 10294

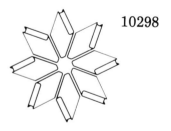 10298

10299

 10295

 10300

 10301

 10302

 10303

10292   Modular Movers
         Designer: Don Connelly & Assocs.

10293   Georgia Journal Of Reading
10293   Georgia Journal of Reading
         Designer: Don Connelly & Assocs.

10294   "LIfetime" Georgia Heart Assn.
         Designer: Don Connelly & Assocs.

10295   Stanley Drugs
         Designer: Don Connelly & Assocs.

10296   Trust Conference
         Designer: Don Connelly & Assocs.

10297   Larkin Coils
         Designer: Don Connelly & Assocs.

10298   Bank Operations School
         Designer: Don Connelly & Assocs.

10299   Video Record Services
         Designer: Don Connelly & Assocs.

10300   Frank Hirt Realty
         Designer: Don Connelly & Assocs.

10301   Reynolds Asphalt Paving
         Designer: Don Connelly & Assocs.

10302   The Palms
         Designer: Don Connelly & Assocs.

10303   The Sails
         Designer: Don Connelly & Assocs.

 10304

 10308

 10305

 10309

 10306

 10310

 10307

10311

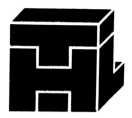 10312

 10313

 10314

10315

10304	Metrocraft Publishing Designer: Don Connelly & Assocs.
10305	The Breakers Designer: Don Connelly & Assocs.
10306	Direct Realty Designer: Don Connelly & Assocs.
10307	Georgia Small Business Assn. Designer: Don Connelly & Assocs.
10308	Baker Graphics Designer: Don Connelly & Assocs.
10309	Low Country Designers Designer: Don Connelly & Assocs.
10310	Folkes Rodeo (Proposed) Designer: Don Connelly & Assocs.
10311	Liberator, Ltd. Designer: Don Connelly & Assocs.
10312	Hampton Townhomes, Ltd. Designer: Don Connelly & Assocs.
10313	The Cocorde Apartments Designer: Richard E. Lyons
10314	Brookstone Apartments Designer: Richard E. Lyons
10315	Buckhead Towne Club Designer: Richard E. Lyons

 10316

 10320

 10321

10317

Laffites

 10318

 10322

 10319

 10323

10324

10325

10326

10327

10328

10332

10329

10333

10330

HIGH ON THE HOG

10334

CELLAR∏SOFTWARE INC.

10331

10335

10336

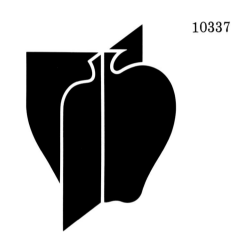

10337

10338

10328 Regency Crown Condominiums
       Designer: Richard E. Lyons

10329 Atlanta Real Estate Appraisal
       Designer: Richard E. Lyons

10330 High On The Hog
       Designer: Jerry Takigawa

10331 River West Medical Center
       Designer: Louis Nelson

10332 Pontiac Land Private, Ltd.
       Designer: Communication Arts Inc.

10333 Anderson Lithograph Company
       Designer: Emmett Morova/
         Douglas Oliver

10334 Celler Software
       Designer: Hester Greene

10335 Lynn Haven
       Designer: Louis Nelson

10336 Arc-en-ciel Foundation
       Designer: Makio Hasegawa

10337 Industrial Designer, Society of
         America
       Designer: Louis Nelson

10338 Tishman West Management
       Designer: Hinsche & Assocs.

10339

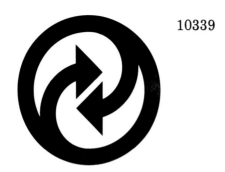

10343

10340

10344

10341

10345

10342

10346

10347

10348

10349

10350

10339 Montreal International Chamber
of Commerce
Designer: Nelu Wolfensohn

10340 El Portal Travel
Designer: Ron Chespak

10341 Don Quarrie
Designer: Douglas Oliver/
Emmett Morova

10342 Sport Specialties Corp.
Designer: Byron Jacobs

10343 Long Beach Chamber of Commerce
Designer: Debra Bradfield

10344 Siena Company
Designer: Communications Arts

10345 Alcohol Awareness Program
Designer: Tishkoff, Wentworth
Associates

10346 Los Angeles Olympic Organizing
Committee
Designer: Keith Bright

10347 Unisource
Designer: Robert Miles Runyan &
Associates

10348 California Restaurants Concepts
Designer: Sachi Kuwahara

10349 Skyline Terrace
Designer: Frank DiNoto

10350 Xerox Corporation
Designer: McElveney & LaMay

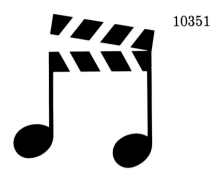

10351

10355

PreferCare Physicians Group

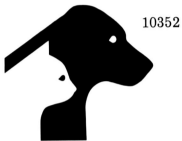

10352

Danbury Animal Welfare Shelter

10356

CALABASH S·E·A·F·O·O·D

10353

10357

10354

CLASSIC DETECTIVES

10358

SM

10359

10360

10361

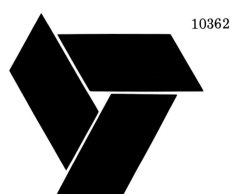

10362

10363

10364

WOODSTREAM
F·A·R·M·S

10365

10366

10367

ICAPITALISM

10368

10369

10370

MEADOWS

10371

PrideAir

10372

Westar

10373

10363   Angeles Corporation
         Designer: Robert Miles Runyan &
           Assoc.

10364   Woodstream
         Designer: Lesniewicz/Navarre

10365   Roach Graphics Inc.
         Designer: Lesniewicz/Navarre

10366   Franklin Park Mall
         Designer: Lesniewicz/Navarre

10367   Integrated Resources
         Designer: Marco DePlano

10368   Texas Federal Services
         Designer: Marc Tedeschi

10369   Eagle Pacific Insurance Co.
         Designer: Jack Anderson

10370   Utex Carpets
         Designer: Dallas Tomlinson &
           Associates

10371   Pride Air
         Designer: Bright & Associates

10372   The Westar Group Ltd.
         Designer: Landor Associates

10373   Gene Bradford
         Designer: Gene Bradford

10374

10378

10375

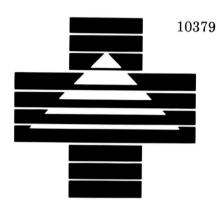

10379

10376

10380

10377

10381

10382

10383

10384

10385

THE PAVILION
INTER·CONTINENTAL SINGAPORE

10374 Fox Hollow Estates
   Designer: Steven Sessions, Inc.

10375 CenTrust
   Designer: Marc Tredeschi

10376 Siesta Key Fitness Center
   Designer: Len Jossel

10377 Creative Alternatives
   Designer: Len Jossel

10378 Ambulatory Surgery Center
   Designer: Len Jossel

10379 Provident
   Designer: Dawayna Perry

10380 Cardoza
   Designer: Jann Church Advtg. &
    Graphics

10381 Provident
   Designer: Jim Sanders

10382 Mobil Land Dvlmnt. Co.
   Designer: Communication Arts
    Inc.

10383 Michael Badger
   Designer: Communication Arts
    Inc.

10384 Okaloosa County Teachers Credit
    Union
   Designer: John H. Harland Co.

10385 Pontiac Land Private, Ltd.
   Designer: Communication Arts
    Inc.

 10386

 10390

10387

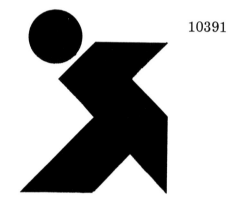 10391

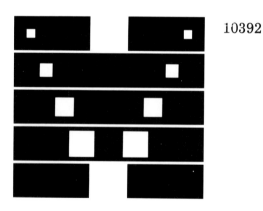 10392

10388

THE VILLAGE OF
PAVOREAL

10389

Age Center

10393

PACIFICA

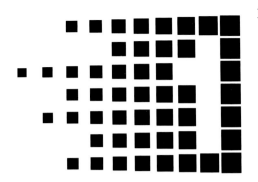

10394

10395

10396

10397

10386 Wiland Services Inc.
Designer: Communication
Arts Inc.

10387 Forma Three Galleries
Designer: Liska & Assocs.

10388 Dick Johnes Dvmnt.
Designer: Thorne, Shepard &
Rodgers

10389 Escajeda
Designer: The Grayson Agency

10390 Balch Springs Bank
Designer: John H. Harland Co.

10391 Harry Stroh Assocs.
Designer: Stephen Longo

10392 Van Horn
Designer: Hornall Anderson Design
Works

10393 Age Center of Worchester, MA
Designer: Blixt & Associates

10394 Cellular One
Designer: Hornall Anderson Design
Works

10395 Tandy Center Ice Rink
Designer: Stan Mancil

10396 Airplane Brokerage & Pilot Instr.
Designer: Stan Mancil

10397 Auto Club
Designer: Stan Mancil

10398

10402

10399

10403

10400

10404

10401

10405

10406

10407

10408

10409

10398	Bookkeeping Firm Designer: Stan Mancil
10399	Coffee Specialty Designer: Stan Mancil
10400	Marriage Enrichment Seminars Designer: Stan Mancil
10401	Texas American Race Teams Designer: Stan Mancil
10402	Fishing Guide For Coastal Waters Designer: Stan Mancil
10403	Grahics West Designer: Stan Mancil
10404	Investment Brokers Designer: Stan Mancil
10405	Bedding & Mattress Co. Designer: Stan Mancil
10406	Exploration Company Designer: Stan Mancil
10407	Hair Cutting Schools & Shops Designer: Stan Mancil
10408	Browns Automotive Repair Shop Designer: Stan Mancil
10409	Greenwood Tucker & Assoc. Golf Course Designers Designer: Stan Mancil

10410

10414

10411

10415

10412

10416

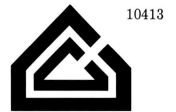

10413

10417

 10418

 10419

 10420

 10421

10410   Limited Additions
        Designer: Stan Mancil

10411   Terry Boyd Investment Firm
        Designer: Stan Mancil

10412   Margaret Kelson Counseling
        Designer: Stan Mancil

10413   The Commercial Companies
        Designer: Stan Mancil

10414   Dallas Post Production Center
        Designer: Stan Mancil

10415   Lee Martin Productions
        Designer: Stan Mancil

10416   Mental Awareness Program
        Designer: Stan Mancil

10417   Stan Mancil Studio
        Designer: Stan Mancil

10418   Alternatives Hair Cutting Shop
        Designer: Stan Mancil

10419   Hair Cutting Shop
        Designer: Stan Mancil

10420   Welborn Mortgage Company
        Designer: Stan Mancil

10421   Welborn & Welborn Insurance Co.
        Designer: Stan Mancil

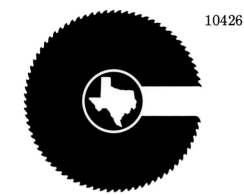

10426

10422

10423

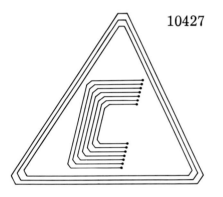

10427

10424

10428

10425

10429

10430

10431

10432

10433

10422	Tom H. Landen Investments Designer: Stan Mancil
10423	SKS Investment Services Co. Designer: Stan Mancil
10424	Gift Shop in California Designer: Stan Mancil
10425	Red Marron Floors, Inc. Designer: Frank Morales
10426	Cold Saws of Texas Designer: Frank Morales
10427	CompuRoute, Inc. Designer: Frank Morales
10428	Solomon Associates, Inc. Designer: Frank Morales
10429	Solomon & Assocs., Inc./Products Designer: Frank Morales
10430	California Dried Figs Designer: Anderson/Miller Comm.
10431	Frances Lux Designer: Frances Lux Des. Studio
10432	Commonwealth of Puerto Rico Designer: Yasumura/CYB
10433	United Brands (Int'l) Corporate System Designer: Yasumura/CYB

 10434

 10438

 10435

 10439

 10436

 10440

10437

10441

10442

10443

10444

10445

10434 Lipton International Players
       Championships
       Designer: J.T. Harding

10435 Tanglewood Mall
       Designer: J.T. Harding

10436 Insurance & Investment Co.
       Designer: J.T. Harding

10437 Interstate Savings & Loan
       Designer: J.T. Harding

10438 J.T. Graphic Design
       Designer: J.T. Harding

10439 Town & Country Linen Corp.
       Designer: Pisarkiewicz Design, Inc.

10440 AmeriHealth, Inc.
       Designer: Young & Martin Design

10441 Redken Laboratories
       Designer: The Van Noy Des. Grp.

10442 Mantegna Inc.
       Designer: Richard Hallam

10443 Hallam Engineering
       Designer: Richard Hallam

10444 Bicoastal Air Service
       Designer: Richard Hallam/
        Walter Dorwin

10445 The Research Corporation
       Designer: Richard Hallam

10446

10450

10447

Exterior Design Service

10451

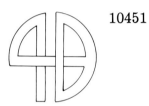

10448

10452

10449

10453

10454

10455

Danielian Associates

10456

HOTEL CONTRACT
DESIGN INC.

10457

10446   Unigene Laboratories
        Designer: Richard Hallam

10447   Exterior Design Service
        Designer: Betty Altherr

10448   Barr Health Institute
        Designer: Betty Altherr

10449   Fairchild Des. & Dvmnt. Inc.
          (Proposed)
        Designer: Deborah Carlson

10450   Fairchild Des. & Dvmnt. Inc.
          (Proposed)
        Designer: Lynn Taylor Brown

10451   Fairchild Des. & Dvmnt. Inc.
          (Proposed)
        Designer: Lynn Taylor Brown

10452   Fairchild Des. & Dvmnt. Inc.
        Designer: Deborah Carlson

10453   Danielian Assocs. (Proposed)
        Designer: Lynn Taylor Brown

10454   Danielian Assocs. (Proposed)
        Designer: Lynn Taylor Brown

10455   Danielian Assocs. (Proposed)
        Designer: Deborah Carlson

10456   Hotel Contract Design, Inc.
        Designer: Lynn Taylor Brown/
          Deborah Carlson

10457   Button-Up Company
        Designer: Lindsay W. Press

10458

10462

10459

10463

10460

10464

10461

10465

 10466

10467

 10468

10469

10458   Interstab Chemical Corp.
         Designer: Hans Boye Boyesen

10459   T. Ohe & Associates, Inc.
         Designer: Marion Flynn

10460   Marion Flynn Graphic Design
         Designer: Marion Flynn

10461   Meredith Corporation
         Designer: Lee & Young

10462   Chicago AMA
         Designer: Donna Pierce

10463   The Market Place Restaurant
         Designer: T.R. Nimen

10464   Michael Kozmiuk, Illustrator
         Designer: T.R. Nimen

10465   Diversified Imports, Inc.
         Designer: William S. Homan

10466   Infobooks Publishing
         Designer: Gloria Garland

10467   Nabisco, Inc.
         Designer: Steven Longo

10468   Sassa's Auto Repair
         Designer: Tom Yasuda

10469   Grant Chemicals Corp.
         Designer: American Media, Inc.

10470   CBS Video
Designer: Alan Peckolick

10471

10472

10471	Tom Erikson Designer: Tom Erickson
10472	Scott Engen, Alpine Ski Instructor Desginer: Scott Engen
10473	Vine-Lore Designer: Scott Engen
10474	Provident Designer: Joyce Mack

10473

10474

Index of Marks

Designers

Abel, Tony & Aldo; 3729 Tamiami Trail, Coral Gables, FL 33134

Adpro Services, Tom Erickson; 1616 Valentia, Denver, CO 80220

American Media; 29 Park Avenue, Rutherford, NJ 07070

Anderson/Miller Communications; 846 California Street, San Francisco, CA 94108

Aucella & Associates; 7 Stuart Place, Westfield, MA 01085

Blixt & Associates; 300 North Fifth, Suite 250, Ann Arbor, MI 48104

Borkowski, Robert; 770-B Washington Road, Pittsburgh, PA 15228

Boye Communications, Inc.; Twenty Park Avenue, Rutherford, NJ 07070

Bradfield Design; 1610 Harper Avenue, Redondo Beach, CA 90278

Bradford, Gene; 13135 Ventura Boulevard, Number 300, Studio City, CA 91604

Bullock, David & Nora; 617 Luella Drive, Kutztown, PA 19530

Burson-Marsteller; 866 Third Avenue, New York, NY 10022

Burson-Marsteller; 1 East Wacker Drive, 16th Floor, Chicago, IL 60601

Carlson & Brown Design Group; 3848 North Campus Drive, Number 110, Newport Beach, CA 92660

Carrier, Catherine; 1019 16th Avenue South, Nashville, TN 37212

Cellular Software, Hester Greene; 43 Great Jones Street, New York, NY 10012

Chavda, Jagdish; P.O. Box 370, Oviedo, FL 32765

Cheltenham, Eugene; 2224 Silver Ridge Avenue, Number 4, Los Angeles, CA 90039

Communication Arts, Inc.; 1112 Pearl Street, Boulder, CO 80302

Connelly, Don; 300 Woodbury Road, Woodbury, NY 11797

Courtland Thomas White, Inc.; 406 West 31st, 12th Floor, New York, NY 10001

Creative Alternatives; 2129 Orchid Street, Sarasota, FL 33579

Dalton, Derek; 334-48 30th Street, Astoria, NY 11106

Design Associates; 2819 Detroit Avenue, Cleveland, OH 44113

Design Directions Inc.; 938 West Cecil Street, Box 454, Neenah, WI 54956

Desginage; 4500 Campus Drive, Suite 210, Newport Beach, CA 92660

Diguiseppe, Nick; American Can Company, Greenwich, CT 06830

Dyer/Kahn, Inc.; 5550 Wilshire Boulevard, Number 301, Los Angeles, CA 90036

Flynn, Marion; P.O. Box 854, Peoria, AZ 85345

Gano Design Associates, 44142 Caminito Islay, San Diego, CA 92122

Garland, Gloria; 24939 Alderbrook Drive, Newhall, CA 91321

Gianninoto Associates; 133 East 54th Street, New York, NY

Ginn, Ken; 3110 Eastside 3, Houston, TX 77098

Gips+Balkind+Associates, Inc.; 244 East 58th Street, New York, NY 10022

Girvin, Tim, Design; 911 Western Avenue, Number 408, Seattle, WA 98104

Hasegawa, Makio; Googolplex+Makio Hasegawa, 711 West End Avenue, 3HN, New York, NY 10025

Gordon, Jim; 6005 Cannon Mountain Drive, Austin, TX 78749

Gorman-Glassberg, Inc., Marco DePlano; 156 Fifth Avenue, Suite 224, New York, NY 10010

Grayson Agency, The; 2455 Juan Street, Suite 360, San Diego, CA 92110

Gruel, Jeff; 1424 Chapala Street, Santa Barbara, CA 93101

Hall, Kevin L.; 406 Woodland Hills Road, White Plains, NY 10603

Hallman, Richard & Walter Dorwin; 345 East 93rd Street, New York, NY 10028

Harding, J.T.; 5 Sentry Lane, Devon, PA 19333

Harland Company; 2329 Miller Road, Decatur, GA 30035

Heiman, Richard, Advertising, Inc., Richard E. Lyons; 3340 Peachtree Road, NE, Atlanta, GA 30326

Hernandez, Nash; 1140 Empire Central Drive, Number 200, Dallas, TX 75247

Hinsche & Associates; 2917 ½ Main Street, Santa Monica, CA 90405

Homan, William S.; 6520 15th Avenue South, Richfield, MN 55423

Hornall Anderson Design Works; 411 1st Avenue South, Suite 710, Seattle, WA 98104

Hull, Steve; 2154 Willowgrove Avenue, Dayton, OH 45409

Humangraphic; 3329 First Avenue, San Diego, CA 92123

Inkwell Advertising, Anton Tielemans; 95 East Tabernacle, St. George, UT 84770

Jasper & Bridge; P.O. Box 388, Kenne Bunk, ME 04043

JD Studios, Jim Dildine; P. O. Box 432, Ft. Walton Beach, FL 32548

Kuntz, Diane; 817 Euclid Street, Santa Monica, CA 90403

Lambert Agency, The; 923 Fremont Avenue, Number 1, South Pasadena, CA 91031

Lavalin; 1130 Sherbrooke West, Montreal, Canada

Lesniewicz/Navarre; 222 North Erie Street, Toledo, OH 43624

Leysen/Johnson Advertising; 883 Production Place, Newport Beach, CA 92663

Lienhart Design; 155 North Harbor Drive, Chicago, IL 60601

Liska & Associates; 213 West Institute, Number 508, Chicago, IL 60610

Longo, Stephen; 2C Colfax Manor, Roselle Park, NJ 07204

Louis Nelson Associates, Melabee Miller; 80 University Place, New York, NY 10003

Lubalin, Peckolick & Associates; 217 East 28th Street, New York, NY 10016

Lux, Frances; 4337 Marina City Drive, Suite 1135 East, Marina Del Rey, CA 90206

Mancil, Stan, Studio; 4908 Locke Street, Ft. Worth, TX 76107

McDonald, Mas, Design Office; 550 North Larchmont Boulevard, Number 202, Los Angeles, CA 90004

McElveney & LeMay; 115 North Union Street, Rochester, NY 14605

Metropolitan Insurance Company; One Madison Avenue, New York, NY 10010

Mickelson Design & Associates; 3906 Minnetonka Avenue, Ames, IA 50010

Miller, Allan & Associates; 1749 Shady Crest Place, El Cajon, CA 92020

Morales Design; 12770 Coit Road, Dallas, TX 75251

Morava & Oliver Design Office; 204 Santa Monica Boulevard, Suite C, Santa Monica, CA 90401

Nimen, T.R.; 447 Pacific Street, Brooklyn, NY 11217

Noeline Pfahler Design; 260 Newport Center Drive, Newport Beach, CA 92660

O'Mara/Seitz Design Group; 1321 7th Street, Number 300, Santa Monica, CA 90401

Odyssey Design Group; 918 F Street, NW, Suite 200, Washington, DC 20004

Our Gang Studios; 3120 St. Mary's Avenue, Omaha, NE 68105

Pace Advertising; 485 5th Avenue, New York, NY 10017

Paxson Advertising; The Landmark Building, Suite 300, San Antonio, TX 78205

Penn Graphics & Design; Box 111, Galeton, PA 16922

Pentagram Design; 212 Fifth Avenue, New York, NY 10010

Perspective Marketers Agency, Ltd.; 1920 Chestnut Street, Suite 903, Philadelphia, PA 19103

Pisarkiewicz Design Inc.; 298 Fifth Avenue, New York, NY 10001

Potts & Plans; Route 10, Box 380, Waco, TX 76708

Press, Lindsay; 27300 Franklin Road, Suite 507, Southfield, MI 48034

Provident Life & Accident Company, Lee Heidel; Fountain Square, Chattanooga, TN 37402

Pullara, Paul; 26 Meadow Drive, Little Falls, NJ 07424

Richards Advertising; 2601 Augusta Drive, Houston, TX 77057

Rousso, Patti/Ed Saunders; 550 Pauyarino, Number G-205, Costa Mesa, CA 92626

Runyan, Robert Miles; 2000 East Culver Boulevard, Playa Del Rey, CA 90293

Sawcheese Studio; 5900 Wilshire Boulevard, Number 1420, Los Angeles, CA 90036

Scrinopskie, Myles J.; 150 Meadow Lane, Topeka, KS 66606

Segura, Carlos M.; 721 Vouray Number B, Kenner, LA 70062

Selwyn Associates, Inc.; 400 College Avenue, Santa Rosa, CA 95401-5120

Seman Graphics; 12 8th Street, Pittsburgh, PA 15222

Sessions, Steven; 4140 SW Freeway, Suite 101, Houston, TX 77027

Silversign; 112 East 19th Street, New York, NY 10003

Smith, Lauren, Design; 2241 Charleston Road, Number 600, Mountain View, CA 94043

Soileau Studio; 3311 Richmond Avenue, Number 315, Houston, TX 77098

Soo Hoo, Patrick; 3757 Wilshire Boulevard, Los Angeles, CA 90010

Southam Associates Inc.; 715 Tatnall Street, Wilmington, DE 19801

Stern, Walter, Consultancy, Ltd., Jay Gold; 514 Ridge Road, Wilmette, IL 60091

Stuart Ford, Inc.; 1108 East Main Street, Richmond, VA 23219

Studiographix; 411 Northgate Plaza, Irving, TX 75062

Takigawa, Jerry; 591 Lighthouse Avenue, Number 27, Pacific Grove, CA 93950

Ten Brink Design; 54 East Swan Street, Columbus, OH 43215

Tharp, Rick; 50 University Number 21, Old Town, Los Gatos, CA 95030

The Map Works, S. Hunter Gordon; 146 3rd Avenue Number 4, Salt Lake City, UT 84103

Thorne, Shepard & Rodgers; 3001 North 2nd Street, Phoenix, AZ 85012

Tishkoff, Wentworth & Associates; 1710 Santa Monica Boulevard, Number 206, Santa Monica, CA 90404

Tomlinson, David; P.O. Box 50942, Randberg, TX

University of Utah, Scott Engen; 207 Milton Bennion Hall, Salt Lake City, UT 84112

Van Noy Design Group; 19750 South Vermont Avenue, Number 200, Torrance, CA 90502

Visual Audibles; 585 West End Avenue, New York, NY 10024

Visual Design Center; 520 North Michigan Avenue, Suite 1230, Chicago, IL 60611

West, Joanne T.; 3605 Northwest Parkway, Dallas, TX 75225

Yasuda Advertising Design; 9527 Caminito Toga, San Diego, CA 92126

Yasumura/CYB; 100 Park Avenue, New York, NY 10017

Young & Martin Design; Atlanta, GA 30305

Zahor Design, Inc.; 150 East 35th Street, New York, NY 10016